# Hurray for Diwali!

Anita Raina Thapan

Illustrated by Alankrita

tota books

HURRAY FOR DIWALI !


Illustrations by Alankrita

First Indian Paperback Edition, 2015

First Reprint, 2016
Second Reprint, 2017
Third Reprint, 2018
Fourth Reprint, 2019
Fifth Reprint, 2021
Sixth Reprint, 2023

ISBN 978-81-7621-200-7

tota books

*Published by* tota books
*An imprint of* **FULL CIRCLE** *PUBLISHING*
J-40, Jorbagh Lane, New Delhi-110003
Tel: 011-24621011
contact@fullcirclebooks.in • www.fullcirclebooks.in



Printed at Ask Advertising Aids Private Limited, New Delhi-110020 India

PRINTED IN INDIA

For Anouka, Zorin, Vani,
Swara and Raagya, who
live in other lands.

May the spirit and joy
of Diwali always be
within you.

Gittoo opened his eyes and stretched his arms. Hmmmm! he smiled with joy. It was the happiest time of the year. The Choti Diwali celebrations were about to begin. Yippee!

Every nook and corner of the house was tidy. The flowerpots had been painted red; the curtains smelled clean and fresh and the floors had been polished.

Now Gittoo could go skating around the house at full speed!

Mama had prepared heaps of sweets - green pista barfis, pink coconut barfis, yellow besan laddoos, white milk cake. There was peanut candy and of course, Gittoo's favourite chocolate fudge!

Gittoo and his elder sister Gauri had been given important work to do...

"You have so many toys, Gittoo, why don't you take out the ones that you don't play with anymore," said Papa. Gittoo found a cricket set that was now too small for him. He would also give away an old Lego set.

"Gauri, why don't you take out some clothes that you have not worn for a while. We will give them away."

Gauri pulled out a pair of jeans and a yellow blouse she was now too tall for.

Soon, they set off for the orphanage with a big basket of fruit and sweets for the children there. It was here that Mama gave away Gittoo's toys and Gauri's clothes.

Meanwhile, Papa was busy wrapping gifts for everyone at home. It had to be done when the children were out of the house, so that it would be a real surprise!

Later that afternoon, Gittoo's cousins from Mumbai, Pia and Chia, Gannu and little Nono Paro, arrived with their parents, Uncle Shyam and Aunty Renu.

It was going to be so much fun together!

To mark Choti Diwali, Mama bought new pans for the kitchen. The children were going to make Kheer for everyone! Gauri boiled the milk, and Pia and Chia took turns to stir the rice in it.

Gittoo and Gannu added the sugar and a few strands of saffron. Little Nono Paro was lifted up so he could sprinkle powdered cardamom into the kheer right at the end.

It looked and smelled delicious!

In the evening, the family gathered in the puja room. Chilbil the cat and Sheru the dog were also present. After all, they too, were family!

Papa lit the lamp in front of the image of Goddess Lakshmi. Mama led the chanting and the family joined in the bhajans.

They said, "We pray to Goddess Lakshmi to bless our home and family with well-being and prosperity."

"What is prosperity?" asked Nono Paro.

"It means having good things to eat everyday," said Gittoo.

"No, it means being healthy and happy," said Gauri.

“For me prosperity is many good books and time to read them,” said Pia.

“I think it means happy holidays with my family every year, and lots of friends,” added Chia.

“But we are only thinking of ourselves!” said Gannu. “Prosperity means that all birds and animals are also happy and that no one ill-treats them ever.”

"Prosperity is all these things," said Mama, "may all human beings, birds, animals and fish be happy. May there be food and good health for all and may Goddess Lakshmi bless everyone big and small."

Then Papa led the aarti and everyone lined up behind him to take turns at waving the lights in front of Goddess Lakshmi.

Soon it was the moment all the children had been waiting for! Each one was given a little Kheer in a bowl.

It was so delicious that everyone asked for second helpings!

The next day many friends visited the house. The postman, the milkman, the gardener, the street sweeper all came and were given Mama's homemade sweets. They also received an envelope each with a little money so that they could buy gifts for their children.

Mama, Aunty Renu and the children worked on the rangoli at the entrance of the house. Like magic, they created intricate designs everywhere.

The next morning dawned; it was finally Diwali! All the children were up early. They couldn't wait for the evening when they would wear their new clothes. Gittoo kept checking the time.

"Mama, are you sure the clock hasn't stopped?" he asked impatiently.

"A little while longer to go, Gittoo" laughed Mama.

"What present am I getting?" asked Gannu.

"Don't be so greedy!" chided Chia.

"Will I also get a present?" inquired Nono Paro who never wanted to be left out!

"Yes," replied Papa. "Everyone will get a present, but only after the puja and after all the lamps have been lit."

All the children gathered around waiting for a story. Mama began, "Diwali is a very special day. Long, long, ago, Lord Rama returned to Ayodhya with his kind queen Sita and his brother Lakshman after fourteen years in the forest. Because Lord Rama was a great and good king, the people had missed him very much while he was away.

When they came home,
everyone was very happy,
they sang and danced,
offered prayers, and lit up
the whole city with lights.”

"Rama returned to Ayodhya after defeating the demon king Ravana," said Gauri who had recently watched the Ramlila.

"Yes, because Ravana had kidnapped Sita and taken her away to Lanka," added Pia.

"That's right," said Mama. "Rama and Lakshman, together with the army of monkeys, defeated Ravana and saved Sita."

"So the lights stand for victory!" exclaimed Gannu.

"It's like when you have a great idea, a light comes on in your brain!" said Gittoo.

"And when you have no ideas, all the lights are switched off in there!" teased Gauri with a giggle.

"Why did Ravana kidnap Sita?" asked Nono Paro.

"Because he thought she was the most beautiful person he had ever seen and he wanted everything good and beautiful for himself!" explained Pia, who always read a lot.

"And it is wrong to take what is not yours!" continued Chia.

"Therefore," said Papa, "we should think before we act. If we keep the light burning bright in our minds, then we won't do things that hurt or upset others."

After the **puja**,
everyone went out
to light the lamps.

As if by magic, the house was transformed into **wonderland**. The lights twinkled like little stars.

It was finally time for presents!

"Ooh, look at my new bag full of lovely hair clips and hair bands," exclaimed Pia.

"Wow!" chimed Gittoo, holding up his new set of paints and colour pencils for all to see.

There was an aeroplane for Nono Paro, a puzzle for Gannu, a cookbook for Gauri and a little tent for Chia. There were even some special dog biscuits for Sheru and a pink collar with a tiny bell for Chilbil.

Then came the crackers. Mama and Papa had said that they would only burn crackers that gave light and which did not make a loud bang, or let out too much smoke.

Everyone played with **phool jhadis**, swirling them around and making the most wonderful patterns in the air.

The **anaars** were like fountains of light scattering little stars and strands of lights all around. Then there were the swirling **chakris** that blazed and dazzled as they swiveled around madly for a few moments of thrill.

Gittoo felt that this was the happiest day of his life.

He caught a glimpse of the biggest earthenware lamp in the puja room still burning bright. He hoped it would continue to burn through the night, and that the Goddess Lakshmi would visit their home and bless it.

He silently made a wish: that everyone in his family would always love each other and that they would always spend Diwali together.

With that, he ran back to join the fun in the garden. There was still a delicious dinner to look forward to!